a year in the life of kew gardens

F
FRANCES LINCOLN LIMITED
PUBLISHERS

a year in the life of kew gardens joanna jackson

Joanna Jackson

To Anne Fraser with thanks for having faith, giving me a chance and changing my life

Acknowledgments:
Thanks to Sue Runyard and Gina Fullerlove at Kew for all their help; Janet Bostock for practising her guiding techniques on me; Steve Frak, my invaluable technical help; and Sue Bishop for her inspirational flower photography.

Frances Lincoln Limited
4 Torriano Mews
Torriano Avenue
London NW5 2RZ
www.franceslincoln.com

A Year in the Life of Kew Gardens
Copyright © Frances Lincoln Limited 2007

Text and photographs copyright © Joanna Jackson 2007

First Frances Lincoln edition 2007

Joanna Jackson has asserted her moral right to be identified as Author of this Work in accordance with the Copyright, Designs and Patents Act 1988.

British Library cataloguing-in-publication data
A catalogue record for this book is available from the British Library

ISBN 978-0-7112-2683-8

Printed in Singapore

PAGE 1 Love-in-a-mist (*Nigella*) seed head
PAGE 2–3 Pots in the fog by the Palm House pond

contents

introduction

For nearly 250 years there has been a botanical garden at Kew. It began as an idea of Prince Frederick, son of George II, and became a reality after his premature death, when his wife, Princess Augusta, assisted by the Earl of Bute, a botanist, set about producing a garden that they hoped would 'contain all the plants known on earth'. Over the years, architects such as Sir William Chambers and Decimus Burton built follies and glasshouses that today are recognized all over the world – in all, there are forty listed structures at Kew and one ancient monument. The gardens also grew considerably in size. Frederick's Kew gardens merged with his parents' Richmond gardens in 1802. In 1840, after the Gardens had fallen into disrepair, the government decided to reinvest in them and Queen Victoria handed them over to the nation. More land was made available and there are now more than 300 acres to care for.

The beautiful grounds are of great historical value, mirroring the development of garden landscaping over the centuries with features such as Capability Brown's Hollow Walk (now the Rhododendron Dell), excavated in 1773, and William Nesfield's great vistas, created in the mid-1800s. These are still very much part of the modern-day design.

Today The Royal Botanic Gardens, Kew, is revered also for its global reputation as a centre for conservation and scientific research. There are as many scientists at Kew as gardeners. The Jodrell Laboratory is responsible for research into a wide variety of plant-related topics. Currently the staff there are working on – among other things – identifying plant-based substances with which to fight illnesses such as cancer, malaria and diabetes, and on DNA barcoding and chemo-taxonomy. The Herbarium contains collections of dried, preserved specimens of plants and fungi. Teams of scientists based at Kew travel all over the world collecting samples of plants, identifying endangered species and providing governments with information so that indigenous flora can be preserved. In times of climate change, when biodiversity is so important, this is vital work.

People have been visiting the Gardens for as long as there have been plants there to see. Attendance figures, which have existed only since 1841, show that numbers peaked in 1915, but fell the next year, when turnstiles were installed and an admission fee charged for the first time. These days more than a million visits are recorded annually. They are vital to the ongoing survival of the Gardens, providing crucial funds, which, together with static funding from the government, are necessary to keep Kew the place it is today.

Rhus reflected in the pond by
the Sir Joseph Banks building

winter

The good thing about a winter visit to Kew is that you can always nip into one of the heated glasshouses to warm up if it gets too chilly or windy outside. Cameras and glasses may steam up, but the respite from the elements is well worth it – as is the amazing array of exotic plants that greets you as you enter. You are transported in an instant from the frozen north to the steamy tropics.

Outside, displays of snowdrops in the Rock Garden and the Queen Charlotte's Cottage ground tell of warmer times to come. In the winter garden by the icehouse the fragrant perfume of viburnum fills the air. The giant compost heap steams as the hot air from the rotting vegetation meets the cold air of winter. The ice rink in front of the Temperate House heaves with activity and a hot chocolate or, better still, a glass of mulled wine is never far away. In January the heady aroma from the witch hazels fills the air around King William's Temple. The holly bushes on the Holly Walk are covered in bright red berries and the Berberis Dell, too, is full of winter berries for the birds. Hellebores cluster around the Ruined Arch and in January and February the silk tassel bush shows off its droopy catkins.

Before Christmas the Gardens are open some evenings, with many of the iconic buildings dramatically lit and specimen trees illuminated. With activities laid on to amuse children, Christmas carols and shopping to entertain adults, what more could you ask for? Who says winter is dull?

Holly Walk:
berries in the snow

royal beginnings

George, Duke of Brunswick-Luneberg, arrived in England from Hanover at the age of fifty-four, unable to speak English and knowing little about the country of which he was about to become king. He was a distant cousin of Queen Anne, and on her death was installed as monarch mainly because of his Protestant faith. Initially he lived with his son, the Prince of Wales (the future George II), in St James's Palace, but the two quickly fell out and his son was banished. The Prince of Wales and his wife, Caroline, moved into Ormonde Lodge in 1718, renaming it Richmond Lodge. The former owner, the Duke of Ormonde, had recently fled the country because of his involvement in the Catholic Jacobite rebellion.

Part of the appeal of Richmond Lodge was its large garden. Caroline particularly loved gardening. She employed Charles Bridgeman and William Kent to landscape the area and set about spending a small fortune on it, building follies such as Merlin's Cave and the Hermitage. As queen she was given an allowance of £100,000 a year – the most a queen had ever been given – yet she still managed to die with debts of £20,000.

True to the Hanoverian tradition, Frederick, first-born son of George II and Caroline, was hated by his parents. He rented the Kew estate, close to Richmond Lodge, possibly in order to annoy his mother and father next door. He employed his mother's favourite architect to modernize the building in Kew that became known as the White House, again probably just to annoy, and when living in Hanover he had taken as his mistress a woman who had served as mistress to both his father and his grandfather. Frederick's irritating behaviour and his popularity with the public fuelled the feud between father and son. It seems ironic that the path that separated the two estates was known as Love Lane. (Later, after the royal period, it became Holly Walk, the prickly plant providing a much more appropriate dividing line.) When Frederick's mother died, she said on her deathbed that she was comforted by the fact that she wouldn't 'have to see that monster again', referring to Frederick.

The pair had one great passion in common, though: their love for gardening. Frederick and his young wife, Augusta, set about transforming the gardens around the White House. The prince was particularly keen on exotic plants. He died prematurely in 1751 before many of his dreams had been realized, his death, according to his doctor, caused by 'contracting a cold by standing in the wet to see some trees planted'. When Frederick died, it was said that 'gardening and planting have lost their best friend'.

The 3rd Earl of Bute, a talented botanist who reputedly had the most 'elegant legs in London', had always spent a lot of time with Augusta, especially when Frederick was off with one of his many mistresses. After Frederick's death Augusta continued to work on the gardens with Bute, amid rumours of an affair. Their mutual love of gardening led to the creation of a botanic garden of nine acres at Kew and thus Augusta is recognized as the originator of the Royal Botanic Gardens, Kew. Frederick's eldest son, the Prince of Wales, was tutored by Bute and the architect Sir William Chambers, from whom Augusta commissioned many buildings for the gardens.

On the death of George II, the Prince of Wales became George III. He married Princess Sophie Charlotte of Mecklenburg-Strelitz in 1761 and three years later Richmond Lodge became the family's summer retreat. 'Capability' Brown was hired as the royal gardener at Hampton Court Palace and commissioned to re-landscape Richmond Gardens. He set about demolishing Merlin's Cave and the Hermitage, removing the riverside terrace and replacing the formal gardens with a more natural landscape. 'When I reflected that he had destroyed that terrace which Queen Caroline made at great expense and pulled down her Merlin's Cave, overturned her Hermitage, filled up her pond, removed her dairy, and drove a plough through her paddock, I own I grieved,' wrote a contributor in the *Middlesex Journal* at the time, expressing a commonly held view. However, opinion was divided: others felt that Brown's work was a great improvement on Caroline's vulgar garden, believing it to be 'a mild agreeable landscape which seems created by the hand of unpresuming taste'. Only the Hollow Walk (now called the Rhododendron Dell) and riverside ha-ha remain of Brown's landscaping.

The death of Augusta in 1772 left the White House free. George III's family was growing rapidly and he had had a major falling out with the Richmond Vestry over a proposed expansion Richmond Lodge – it had refused him permission to buy more land. In a fit of pique he moved to the White House in Kew and moved the Prince of Wales and his brother Frederick into the Dutch House (now known as Kew Palace) opposite. For three months each year they all played happy families at Kew, away from the affairs of state.

Queen Caroline had kept a menagerie in Richmond Gardens, which included in its collection tigers. Queen Charlotte converted what was possibly the menagerie keeper's cottage into the Queen's Cottage (now known as Queen Charlotte's Cottage) in the *cottage orné* style of rustic simplicity fashionable at the time. The family used the cottage for picnics and a new menagerie was built near by to house kangaroos, newly discovered and brought over from Botany Bay. In Kew's heritage year wallabies were present in an enclosure near the cottage on the site of the original.

In 1788 George III suffered his first spell of illness from the genetic condition porphyria and he was confined to Kew. When he recovered, he decided to build a new palace 200 yards away on the riverside opposite Brentford. By 1800 costs for this new castellated palace were escalating. The king became ill again and lost interest in the project and the building was halted, with the palace only partially built. The family were now squashed into the Dutch House, the White House having been demolished to provide building materials for the new home. Space must have been at a premium because by now there were fifteen children in the family. The seventeenth-century Tompian sundial today situated in front of Kew Palace was erected by George IV and marks the site of the White House.

The king's episodes of mental disturbance increased in frequency and Kew grew to symbolize imprisonment and suffering for him, as he was always confined there when ill. He went permanently mad in 1810 and George, Prince of Wales, was made regent in 1811. The queen became fat and bad-tempered, probably as a result of the depression that followed her husband's demise. She died in the Dutch House in 1818.

During George III's reign the Kew and Richmond Gardens were merged and Richmond Lodge was demolished. Sir Joseph Banks, a renowned botanist, became the unofficial first director of Kew from 1773. He increased the Gardens' collection and spent much of his own money on bringing new plant species to them.

In 1820 both George III and Sir Joseph Banks died. George IV ordered the demolition of the embarrassing, eccentric edifice that was the castellated palace. This proved to be easier said than done. Eventually the place had to be blown up because its infrastructure of cast iron was so sturdy.

George IV had little interest in Kew and in 1826 it was said, 'Kew unquestionably possesses the most complete collection of exotic plants in Europe but it is rather neglected.' The two gardens had always been open to the public, Kew on Thursdays or Mondays and Richmond on Sundays, from June through to September. However, when William IV came to the throne he stopped all that.

Although she spent time at Kew as a child, Queen Victoria had little interest in the Gardens and as a result of a royal commission in 1840 the Gardens were handed over to the nation and Sir William Hooker was appointed the first official Director and the Gardens' fortunes began to improve once again. Augusta's legacy lived on.

Dante's inferno or the compost heap at Kew?

One of the two Chinese lions
by the Palm House Pond in
December fog

A gull sits on the roof of the
Palm House.

Wounded Angel sculpture in
front of the Temperate House

King William's Temple in the snow

The Queen's Beasts

The Pagoda from the
Cedar Vista

The Syon Vista

Hercules Wrestling the River-god
Achelous on the Palm House Pond

Hellebores by the Ruined Arch

The Princess of Wales
Conservatory and the Orangery,
beautifully lit at Christmas

A seed head of *Pulsatilla* in the Rockery

A heron rests on a rowing boat on the Palm House Pond.

Snow covers the cones and fir trees by the Lake at the north end of the Cedar Vista.

Swans trying to keep warm floating like icebergs around the Lake

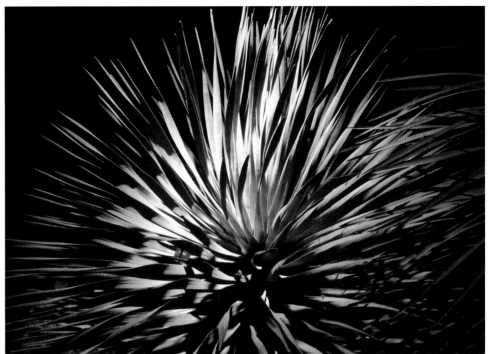

A *Dracaena cinnabari* beautifully lit in the Princess of Wales Conservatory

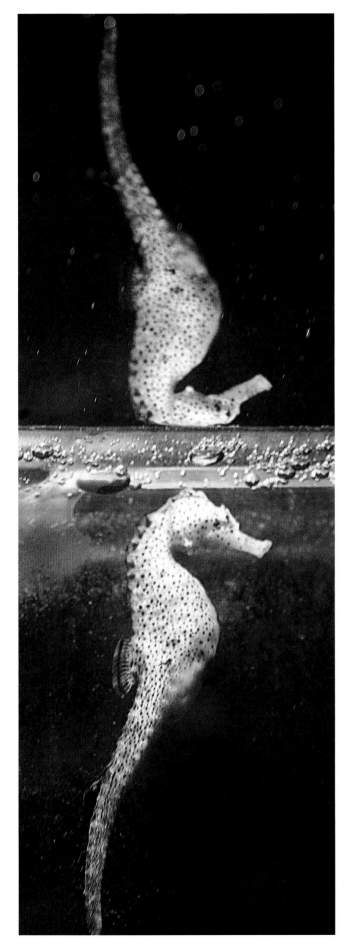

A seahorse and its reflection in the Marine Display in the basement of the Palm House

Frosted common ivy by King William's Temple

The elegant roofs of White Peaks

Frost and mist on a winter's morning in the Arboretum

The Palm House at sunrise

Heavenly scented witch hazel (in
front of the Temple of Aeolus)

The oriental plane tree, one of the 'Old Lions' planted in 1762, in front of Kew Palace

Snowdrops in the wild Conservation Area in the south corner of the Gardens

Orchids on display in the
Princess of Wales Conservatory
(above) and Nash Conservatory
(left) in February during the
Orchid Festival. Alien invasion or
orchid detail?

spring

It has been said that spring is nature's way of saying 'Let's party'. Walk around Kew in spring and you would have to agree. As you enter through Victoria Gate, you are greeted by one and a half million purple and white cultivated crocuses. Waves of less showy but subtly beautiful wild crocuses are found throughout the Arboretum. When you have had enough of crocuses, you can move on to daffodils. The Broad Walk is a mass of yellow and other areas in front of White Peaks and the Princess of Wales Conservatory are also carpeted in a 'host of golden daffodils'. The heavily scented Lilac Garden is full of bloom, as are the nearby magnolias and azaleas. On the ground, clusters of beautiful snake's head fritillaries bob their heads up and down. In front of the Temperate House the Cherry Walk is full of cherry blossom and below the cherry trees the myriad blue flowers of 300,000 scillas cover the ground. For more blue experiences, go to the Conservation Area to see thousands of wild bluebells around Queen Charlotte's Cottage. In front of the Palm House the formal beds are a riot of colour, tulips and primroses providing the cabaret at this time.

A walk around the Gardens in spring is a truly uplifting experience: they really are a joy to behold.

Bluebell in the Conservation Area

LEFT A mallard hides in
the bluebells in the
Conservation Area.

RIGHT Bluebells by the
Badger Set

Queen Charlotte's Cottage is
surrounded by bluebells in
the spring.

marianne north

British history is littered with tales of eccentric adventurers who explored and discovered new things. Such a person was Marianne North. Never fitting in to the stereotype of the Victorian lady, she wandered the globe alone, taking risks for the sake of her dual passions of plants and painting.

She was born 24 October 1830 in Hastings into a wealthy, political family. Her father was Frederick North, MP, and her mother the daughter of Sir John Marjoribanks, another MP. Her formative years included many periods of travelling. Whenever her father failed to win a seat at a general election the family set off on an extended trip around Europe. Those days were times of unrest and the family had to make hasty exits from both Vienna and Dresden to avoid being involved in riots.

As a youngster, Marianne was obsessed not with horticulture but with music; it was not unknown for her to practise playing the piano and singing for eight hours a day. She tended to pursue solitary interests, preferring riding, singing and painting to socializing. Her father, however, had many distinguished acquaintances and introduced Marianne to many influential people from the scientific, artistic, literary and political worlds. Sir William Hooker, Director of Kew, was a particular friend. Marianne was taken to Kew many times and developed an interest in plants and a desire to go to the tropics to see plants she had seen in the glasshouses at Kew in their natural environment.

When Marianne was thirty-nine her father died. He had been her beloved companion and she was distraught after his death. She had no intention of ever marrying, describing the institution as 'a terrible experiment'. She lived miserably in England for almost two years after her father's death and then received an invitation to visit America. So began the most adventurous part of her life; for Marianne 'life truly did begin at forty'. For the next thirteen years she travelled the world, painting plants in their natural setting. She started in North America and Jamaica and then headed south to Brazil. She moved on to the Far East, visiting Japan, Borneo, Java and Ceylon. She spent 1878 in India

and on her return had a successful exhibition in London. This prompted her to offer her paintings and a building to house them to Kew Gardens for permanent viewing. Kew accepted her generous offer and the architect James Fergusson, her friend, designed a colonial-style house, inspired by her Indian experience and by his interest in the lighting of Greek temples.

Work began on the house, but before it was completed Marianne was off again. She followed Charles Darwin's advice by visiting Australia and New Zealand. In 1882 the Marianne North Gallery was opened. It subsequently had to be enlarged when trips to South Africa, the Seychelles and Chile produced more paintings.

Eventually ill health curtailed Marianne's gallivanting and she died in 1890. Her sister edited her journals and published two volumes under the title *Recollections of a Happy Life*. These proved so popular that she published a further volume, *Further Recollections of a Happy Life*.

The gallery at Kew remains a testament to this prodigious painter. A space she conceived, helped design, paid for and filled with her life's work, it is a fitting tribute to a remarkable woman.

New shoots of the American red
oak (*Quercus rubra*) by the Pagoda

Frost covers the Syon Vista.

A gentle breeze sets free a cloud of pollen from the *Torreya californica* in the Woodland Glade.

43

the palm house

LEFT The Palm House

RIGHT Flower pots in the Palm House

By 1841 when Sir William Hooker became the first official director of the Royal Botanic at Gardens at Kew, the Gardens had considerably increased in size and public access had recently been granted. Botanical expeditions to far-flung corners of the world had provided the Gardens with many exotic plants. It was decided that a prestigious glasshouse should be built to house these new acquisitions and provide a showcase to please the ever-growing number of visitors.

Greenhouses had been around since AD 30, when the Roman Emperor Tiberius was told by his doctors to eat a cucumber a day to stay healthy and, in order to provide him with his daily vegetable all year round, a *specularium* was built. This structure had a glass-like covering of translucent sheets of mica, and was wheeled outside during the day and brought in again at night. The first practical greenhouse is credited to the French botanist Jules Charles, who in 1599 built a glass structure in Leiden in the Netherlands to grow medicinal tropical plants. The idea of growing plants under glass spread and the French, who had a love of a new fruit, the orange, began building orangeries to protect their orange trees from frost. Experimenting with angled glass walls and heating flues went on throughout the seventeenth century. It was, however, the Victorian age, when the Industrial Revolution brought technical advances, that was the golden era of the greenhouse. Kew benefited from the newfound knowledge.

Hooker employed the architect Decimus Burton and the Irish iron founder Richard Turner to collaborate to build the new Palm House. Burton acknowledged Turner's technical competence, but he disapproved of his 'ecclesiastical', over-elaborate ornamentation, preferring a style of purity and simplified form. It was not a marriage made in heaven, but the two men overcame their differences to produce in 1844–8 what is considered to be the finest example of a Victorian glasshouse in the world. Burton's simple design has been softened by touches added by Turner such as sculptured sunflowers on the internal ironwork.

Hooker wanted a large space in the middle of the building in which to place the tallest palms that Kew possessed. Borrowing engineering ideas from shipbuilding, Turner built the Palm House like an upturned ship's hull. He used the latest materials, including the strong, workable and most importantly light wrought iron, to make the delicate ribs across a span of fifty feet with no supporting pillars, which was unheard of at the time. Below the main building was a basement containing boilers that provided the heat to warm up the glasshouse to the appropriate temperature. The smoke generated was piped away 500 feet to the chimney, which was disguised as an Italian Romanesque campanile.

The Palm House was built on the swampy land that was once part of the lake. The curator John Smith had warned of the risk of flooding, but his sensible words went unheeded. He was proved correct very soon in 1848, when the basement flooded and subsequently pumps had to be used to keep the basement dry.

The glass was originally green, as it was believed that the sun would scorch the plants if clear glass was used. This was the time of the Industrial Revolution, though, when pollution from smoke was common, and the windows became so black with soot that little light could penetrate. Gradually the green glass was replaced by clear glass. It was also becoming understood that humidity more than light was the biggest factor involved in successfully keeping exotic plants alive.

By the 1950s the Palm House was in a state of disrepair. It was closed to the public from 1952 and restored in 1955–7. By the early 1980s it was obvious that the building had become unsafe again and something drastic had to be done. In 1984 the house was totally cleared of plants for the first time in its history. It was virtually dismantled and over the next five years rebuilt, using toughened glass and ten miles of stainless-steel glazing bars. The basement was converted into the Marine Display and modern heating mechanisms were introduced. The fabric of the building had to be preserved, though, because it is a Grade I listed building. The Palm House was reopened to the public by the Queen Mother in November 1990.

The Palm House contains plants from tropical rainforest worldwide, with the south wing containing African flora, the north wing Asian, Australian and Pacific flora and the central area American flora and giant palms. Among the African collection is one of the oldest pot plants in the world. This is a cycad, *Encephalartos altensteinii*, brought to Kew in 1775. Many economically important plants are present, labelled with educational plaques explaining their role in the world today. These include coffee, which is the second most important commodity on the world market after oil.

the hooker dynasty

By the late-1830s Kew was falling into disrepair through neglect and lack of funding following the deaths of George III and Sir Joseph Banks, who had run Kew for almost half a century. The government dithered about its future. Invest and expand or close it and disperse the plants were the two choices on offer. Luckily for us, because of pressure from scientists the government agreed to keep the Gardens open and improve them. In 1841 Sir William Hooker was employed as the first full-time Director of Kew Gardens.

Sir William Hooker was born in Norwich in 1785. He was wealthy enough to indulge in his hobby and passion, the study of natural history, specializing in botany. He made his first botanical expedition to Iceland at the suggestion of Sir Joseph Banks. After several more plant-collecting expeditions, he settled in Suffolk and devoted himself to the formation of his herbarium, which became renowned worldwide among botanists. In 1820 he became Professor of Botany at the University of Glasgow and worked to lay out and develop the Glasgow Botanic Gardens. As director of Kew he had a profound impact on the development of the gardens. He was by all accounts a charming man and used all his social skills to keep all the varying interested parties happy.

Hooker opened the Gardens to the public every weekday afternoon, and visitor numbers increased from 9,174 in 1841 to 28,139 in 1845. Prior to his appointment the collection was guarded jealously, but he willingly swapped seeds and plants with other gardens, thus greatly increasing the number and variety of species at Kew. Until then the Botanic Gardens had been separate from the rest of the gardens, the Pleasure Grounds, but Hooker needed more space for the ever-expanding plant collection and was granted the old Pleasure Grounds and an extra 46 acres. These additions increased the area of land available from 11 to 274 acres.

With the able assistance of the architect Decimus Burton and landscape designer William Nesfield, Hooker transformed Kew into a place not dissimilar to the Kew we know today. Nesfield created three great vistas, including those to Syon House and the Pagoda, along with the Broad Walk. The Palm House and Temperate House were built, new main gates were added, a flagpole erected and the Museum of Economic Botany and the Herbarium established. When Hooker died in 1865, the Kew he had taken over was unrecognizable: the neglected garden had become a botanic garden of immense national importance.

On Hooker's death in 1865 he was succeeded by his son Sir Joseph Hooker. Joseph was himself a brilliant scientist who had attended his father's lectures at the University of Glasgow from the age of seven. Unlike his father, he did not have the luxury of an independent income and worked as an assistant surgeon on HMS *Erebus*, spending years exploring the Southern Ocean and collecting plants. He went on to collect plants in Australia, India and the Himalayas. He became a highly regarded botanist with a worldwide reputation but continued to find paid work difficult to come by. His father secured him the post of assistant director of Kew in 1855, the appointment no doubt helped by William's offer to bequeath his vast herbarium to the gardens.

Whereas Sir William had been a diplomat in his dealings with people his son was a rather spiky character. One of his best friends, Charles Darwin, described him as 'impulsive and somewhat peppery in temper'. One subject guaranteed to rouse him was public access to the Gardens. He believed that the Gardens' prime objective was to be a scientific establishment, not a recreational area. He complained vociferously about the 'mere pleasure of recreation seekers whose motives are rude rompings and games'. He also came to blows with the Natural History Museum over the ownership of the Herbarium. After prominent men of science, including Darwin, had backed him, the Herbarium remained at Kew.

Sir Joseph Hooker remained Director of Kew for twenty years. These years were ones of consolidation of his father's work and an increase in Kew's scientific credentials. One of his

Three hundred thousand scillas
provide a carpet of blue in front
of the Temperate House.

finest achievements was the setting up of the Jodrell Laboratory. He retired in 1885 and was succeeded by his son-in-law Sir William Thistelton-Dyer.

Thistelton-Dyer was as combative as his father-in-law and even more eccentric. He had started his academic life studying maths at Oxford and later turned to natural sciences, becoming for a period Professor of Botany at the Royal College of Science in Dublin. He took up the post of Assistant Director at Kew under Sir Joseph in 1875. During his tenure as Director he reorganized Kew's administration and ran Kew much more efficiently than it had been before. Much of his work was devoted to the colonies

and economic botany: for instance, it was he who introduced rubber from Brazil to the plantations of Malaya and Sri Lanka. He was responsible for the first Alpine House and he completed the building of the Temperate House, which became the largest glasshouse in the world. One of his eccentricities was an obsession with uniforms. He was the first to employ female gardeners but insisted they wear 'brown bloomers and thick woollen stockings' so as not to encourage 'sweethearting'.

The Hooker dynasty lasted from 1840 to 1905 and between them they had an enormous influence on the development of Kew.

A few of the two million crocuses
blooming in the Gardens in spring

Crocus detail

The Broad Walk, awash with daffodils

A statue named *Out in the Fields* in
the Order Beds. Daffodils in the
Secluded Garden and in front of the
Princess of Wales Conservatory

A replica of Verrochio's *Boy with a Dolphin* stands in front of the magnificent laburnum arch in the Queen's Garden.

The spiral staircase in the
Temperate House

The balcony of the Palm House
and a copy of Donatello's *David*
in the Temperate House

Tree ferns in the New Zealand area of the Temperate House

61

Magnolias, lilac and cherry blossom flourish in the spring sunshine. Cherry blossom petals rest on a mossy tree trunk.

LEFT Snake's head fritillary.
Thousands are planted between
the Lilac Garden and the
magnolia collection.

RIGHT The waterfall in the Rockery
by the Davies Alpine House

RIGHT Statue entitled *Autumn*,
near the Temperate House.

summer

Summer at Kew is a time for lazy strolls, relaxing in the shade of the trees in the Arboretum, taking in the scent of the philadelphus by the Pagoda and having a cooling drink outside one of the cafés. The warm days mean enjoying what the Gardens have to offer at a leisurely pace, with lots of stops to admire the lovely surroundings. Things to enjoy include the Duke's Garden with its Lavender Trail; wandering under the Rose Pergola while looking admiringly at the students' vegetable plots and the groups of related flowers in the Order Beds; the colour spectrum, with flowers of many hues that will give the avid gardener inspirational ideas to try out at home on a smaller scale; and the tranquil Waterlily Pond, where male peacocks strut their stuff with their magnificent tails in full decorative order. In front of the Palm House over-the-top blowsy arrangements fill the formal flower beds and behind is the Rose Garden, full of an array of roses of all shapes, sizes, colours and scents.

In midsummer the Gardens come alive in the evenings to the sound of music provided by bands performing at the Summer Swing Music festival. Hordes arrive with their fancy picnics for an outdoor extravaganza, and linger until dusk brings dramatic firework displays to end the evening's entertainment.

Sunflower

evolution of plants

Once a seething inferno of volcanic activity, our planet gradually calmed down and began to cool, becoming a collection of sterile, barren land masses surrounded by water. All life on earth as we experience it today evolved from that water.

Conditions were perfect for the development of the first organisms on earth. These were the cyanobacteria, or blue-green algae. These single-celled organisms, with the help of sunlight, combined carbon dioxide and water to produce oxygen – a process known as photosynthesis. For 1,500 million years these organisms remained in the sea, because the land was bathed in lethal levels of ultra-violet radiation and totally inhospitable. Gradually, though, as the algae spewed out oxygen, the amount of the gas in the atmosphere became large enough to form an ozone layer, which blocked out the sun's most harmful rays. This allowed the algae to venture on to land.

These plants had to be adaptable and prepared to survive periods of drying out as the sea ebbed and flowed with the tide. They became known as seaweeds. Mosses, lichens and liverworts also evolved on the land. Like the algae, they were reliant on moisture to survive and reproduce, and their growth was limited because they had no vascular system with which to conduct water through their bodies. The horsetails, club mosses and ferns came next. They had developed a vascular system, by which fluid was transported up and down the plant via tubular structures in the roots and stems. Some of these plants grew to a height of 30 metres.

The world's climate was then mild and the land was warm and swampy. Forests of horsetails and ferns flourished. But when the land started to dry out and the temperature began to drop, the earliest forests began to die back. Their need for a moist environment in which to reproduce was holding plants back.

At that time conifers, cycads and ginkgos began to evolve and with them the production of seeds. Seeds contain a young plant and a nutrient store. This means that they can colonize areas with transient water supplies, by lying dormant until the required conditions prevail.

In the animal kingdom insects were evolving and living in harmony with plants, feeding on them and ultimately being used by the plants in the fertilization process. This is co-evolution, whereby two or more interdependent species each adapt to changes in one another. It led to plants developing flowers with perfumes, colours and nectar to lure insects towards the pollen within a plant so that they would become dusted with the pollen and transfer it to the next flower when they moved on, thus pollinating the flower and enabling fertilization to take place. The problem with this system, though, was that insects went from one type of flower to another indiscriminately. In order to ensure the transfer of pollen to the right species, the plants therefore had to make the process more species specific, adapting so that particular insects would be interested only in particular flowers. Orchids are some of the most highly adapted flowers. Some orchids attract insects by sexual impersonation: the flower resembles a female wasp, complete with eyes, antennae and wings, and even gives off the odour of a female wasp in mating condition.

At Kew it is possible to see all stages of the evolutionary progress of plants. The Evolution House takes you through the earliest years with a Marine Display that shows plants living in the sea and its margins. Conifers and ginkgos can be found in the grounds, while cycads and ferns are in the glasshouses. Flowers in their myriad forms are all over the place. Orchids are to be found in the Princess of Wales Conservatory, where in February there is an annual festival of tropical plants.

The Sackler Crossing and the
Waterlily Pond

The Lake after a fierce summer
thunderstorm

A bee digs around for pollen in a
giant thistle in the Secluded Garden.

A dramatic firework display ends
an evening of music at the
Summer Swing Festival.

Lavender in front of the Princess
of Wales Conservatory

The rose arbour and rose detail
in the Order Beds

Boy with a dolphin in the fountain
in the Queen's Garden behind
Kew Palace

Kew Palace, seen from the
Colour Spectrum

Echinacea detail

sir william chambers and the pagoda

Sir William Chambers was born in Sweden in 1723 and later educated in England. His first employment was with the Swedish East India Company, which required him to travel to Bengal and Canton. While in China he studied and sketched Chinese architecture, and he returned to England with a sound knowledge of the fashionable chinoiserie. After his stint with the East India Company he studied architecture and was appointed architectural tutor to the future George III and architect to George's mother, Princess Augusta, who is commonly credited with the creation of Kew.

Chambers's most famous building is Somerset House and typically his designs were of a restrained Palladian style. However, in the middle of the eighteenth century it became very fashionable for the rich and famous who could afford it to have decorative buildings and follies built on their estates, and Princess Augusta employed Chambers to design such items for her gardens at Kew. He was given the freedom to indulge his fantasies and designed twenty-five exotic buildings. Today, five remain: the Orangery, the Ruined Arch, the Temple of Bellona, the Temple of Aeolus and his most iconic structure, the Pagoda.

The Pagoda was completed in 1762. It is 50 metres/163 feet tall, which means it is visible from outside the gardens. Horace Walpole wrote to a friend at the time of the construction, 'We begin to perceive the tower of Kew from Montpelier Row: in a fortnight you will be able to see it in Yorkshire.' It has ten storeys, all octagonal, and each successive level gradually diminishes in size. Apparently, though, to be an authentic copy it should have had an odd number of floors.

Originally the building was adorned with dragons – eighty of them in all, covered in glass and brightly coloured. Decimus Burton suggested in 1843 that the dragons should be fully restored but the cost – £4,350 – ruled this idea out.

During the Second World War holes were made in the floors so that bomb designers could drop models from top to bottom to study their flight. The Pagoda survived the Blitz, despite having a few narrow escapes from German bombs dropping in the vicinity.

The Pagoda was closed for many years, but it was renovated in 2005 and reopened to the general public for Kew's heritage festival in 2006. You stagger up the nine flights of stairs to experience fabulous views of the Gardens and the surrounding countryside and cityscape.

Sunset over the Lake

Students' vegetable plots

Water trickles down the sculpture
in the Secluded Garden.

The sun setting over the River
Thames, as seen from the end
of the Lake in the north-west
of the Gardens

Giant waterlily leaves in the
Waterlily House

LEFT Sprinklers provide humidity in the Palm House and a heron rests on the bridge across the pond by the Sir Joseph Banks Building.

RIGHT Vibrant colours in the Colour Spectrum and looking across to the Orangery

autumn

The 'Season of mists and mellow fruitfulness' brings with it dew-laden spiders' webs, a multitude of mushrooms and toadstools as well as the browning of the leaves on the trees. The obvious place to be at this time of year is the Arboretum. The trees give a grand finale before retiring for the winter. The maples and acers blaze red, the smoke bush by Victoria Gate glows orange and the maidenhair tree by the Princess of Wales Conservatory shows off its bright yellow foliage. On a still day the reflections of the larch in the Lake are spectacular and the squirrels busy themselves collecting chestnuts for their winter pantries. On the ground, colour is provided by autumn crocuses near White Peaks and hardy cyclamen put on a show under the hornbeams in the Queen's Garden. There is usually a display of pumpkins and squashes by the Waterlily House and in 2006 the lake in front of the Palm House was awash with bright pink cranberries – there is always something new and interesting to see. The berries begin to appear on the berberis and holly bushes, providing a multitude of birds with a good meal. If it gets a bit nippy while you are wandering around, why not pop into one of the glasshouses to warm up and have a look around at the exotic plants they contain? Chillies are fruiting in the Temperate House at this time of year; see them and transport yourself to a hot Mexican beach before heading out once again into the beautiful British autumn at Kew.

Autumn crocus by White Peaks

Condensation runs down the
doors of the Palm House.

economic botany

The majority of European botanic gardens began life as physic gardens, where plants were grown for their healing properties and studied for the furtherance of medical knowledge. In the early 1700s, though, botanic gardens began to be used for economic reasons. In Amsterdam, for instance, economic crops were grown for use in the Dutch Colonies.

When Sir Joseph Banks began to have influence at Kew, he transformed it from a royal hobby into a centre for the global transfer of plants, particularly to botanic gardens in the rapidly expanding British colonies. This role was to prove very useful to Britain commercially in the future. Banks dispatched explorers and botanists around the world to look for new plants, including economically useful species that could be grown in the diverse climates and environments over which the British ruled.

One trip Banks helped organize was William Bligh's infamous voyage on HMS *Bounty*, now better known for its mutiny. Bligh's mission had been to collect breadfruit from Tahiti for cultivation in the West Indies to help feed the growing slave population there. The slaves had been brought from Africa to work on the sugar cane plantations of the Caribbean. By transplanting species to different countries and continents, Banks changed entire landscapes. Probably his greatest legacy was his exchange of many plants between the old and new worlds.

After Sir Joseph Banks died, Kew deteriorated and by the time Sir William Hooker took over as Director in 1841 no Kew collectors were working abroad. Hooker recognized the importance to the economy and the colonies of collecting and distributing plant species. In his reports of 1849 and 1850 he commented on how useful it was to introduce plants 'in commerce, in medicine, in agriculture and domestic economy' and wrote, 'It has indeed been our special object to cultivate what may be useful and valuable to our colonies.'

Hooker's most famous movement of species was that of cinchona from South America to India. At the beginning of the seventeenth century French chemists had discovered how to extract quinine from the bark of the trees and use it to help treat malaria. This discovery was highly important to all European countries with colonies in the tropics, where malaria was prevalent. Annual expenditure on quinine for the British army in Bengal alone exceeded £40,000, a fortune in those days, so it was imperative to manufacture it locally at vastly reduced cost. Kew sent collectors to transport cinchona trees from the Amazon to the East and sent botanists with the seedlings to use their expertise to establish plantations. It was noted that 'the records of the Colonial and India Offices will show of what immense importance the establishment of Kew has been to the welfare of the entire British Empire.'

Rubber was another crop Kew was to be hugely influential in establishing in Asia. Latex, the milky juice of rubber trees, had been known about since Columbus's voyage to the Americas in 1493 but it remained nothing more than a novelty until the mid-nineteenth century, when Nelson Goodyear invented vulcanization, a treatment that turned latex into a tough and durable material. Consequently, Brazilian rubber seeds and cuttings were successfully transported via Kew to Sri Lanka, Singapore and Malaysia. A rubber boom followed John Dunlop's marketing of the pneumatic tyre in 1888. British plantations there thrived on the proceeds of not only rubber production but coffee and tea as well, with Kew providing the expertise needed to keep the plants healthy.

At the turn of the twentieth century the British Empire began to break up and many of the colonies started to become self-governing, developing their own agricultural specialists and research facilities. Kew's role accordingly began to change. Today conservation and sustainable use of plants, along with research into new medicines, are Kew's scientific priorities.

In 1848 Sir William Hooker set up at Kew the first museum of economic botany in the world. Its purpose was to demonstrate the importance of plants to mankind. A building opposite the Palm House, now known as Museum No. 1, was built in 1857

Museum No.1 and cranberries.
A coot enjoys the influx of cranberries.

especially to display an ever-expanding collection of useful plants and products. Today this building is the home of the Plants+People exhibition, which is a fascinating look at how plants are important in every aspect of our lives, including the clothes we wear, the food we eat, the fuel we use and the medicine we take. They are so much more than just beautiful things to look at.

the japanese at kew

In 1910, a Japanese–British exhibition was held at White City in London. It was the largest international exhibition the empire of Japan had ever participated in, driven by the Japanese desire to develop a more favourable public image in Great Britain. Part of the exhibition was a Japanese garden that was constructed from scratch at the exhibition site. Authenticity was of the utmost importance and trees, shrubs, buildings, bridges and stones were all shipped over from Japan. Over 8 million people visited the exhibition and it was considered very successful. After it was over the model of the Gateway of the Imperial Messenger, or Chokushi-mon, was transferred to the botanic gardens at Kew, where it has remained ever since.

The Chokushi-mon is a four-fifths-size replica of the Karamon of Nishi Hongan-ji in Kyoto, the ancient imperial capital of Japan. The original was built in the late sixteenth century and this copy is considered the finest example of a traditional Japanese building in

Detail in the Japanese Garden

Europe. Over the years it fell into disrepair but it was fully restored in 1995, the work having taken a year to complete. The only alteration was the removal of the old lead-covered cedar bark roof shingles. They were replaced by longer-lasting copper tiles.

The area around the gateway is known as the Japanese Landscape, comprising three traditional Japanese gardens representing peace, activity and harmony. The gravel and rocks in front of the building represent the vigorous flowing movement of water down hillsides and over waterfalls. The landscape includes two of the fifty Kurume azalea cultivars introduced to the Western world by the plant collector E.H. Wilson.

The Japanese festival of 2001 saw the addition of another Japanese building to the Kew landscape: the Minka House. Rescued by the Japan Minka Reuse and Recycle Association, the house was dismantled in Japan, where it was lived in until 1993, and shipped to Kew. It was rebuilt by Japanese carpenters, and a team of British builders who had previously worked on the Globe Theatre and were skilled in building wattle-and-daub walls.

Minkas were the houses of choice for a large proportion of the country population in Japan up until the mid-twentieth century. They were very practical, as they were earthquake resistant and if damaged could be easily repaired using natural materials. In the north they were built with steep roofs to cope with long, snowy winters and in the south they had raised floors to withstand the frequent typhoons. Modern houses, although more comfortable to live in, are not so ecologically sound and the Japan Minka Reuse and Recycle Association was established to promote the benefits and conservation of Minka houses.

The Minka House is situated among the bamboos of the Bamboo Garden. Bamboos are members of the grass family and there are over 1,000 different species worldwide. Like other grasses, if neglected they can become very invasive over time. The different types in the Bamboo Garden are contained by heavy-duty recycled rubber, which provides a physical barrier to their spreading habit. Bamboo is often present in Japanese gardens, grown for its graceful form and foliage and for the rustling of the leaves when the wind blows.

The Lake

The Temple of Bellona

A peacock perches on top of the roof of the toilet block near the Waterlily Pond.

White Peaks and the Palm
House, at sunset

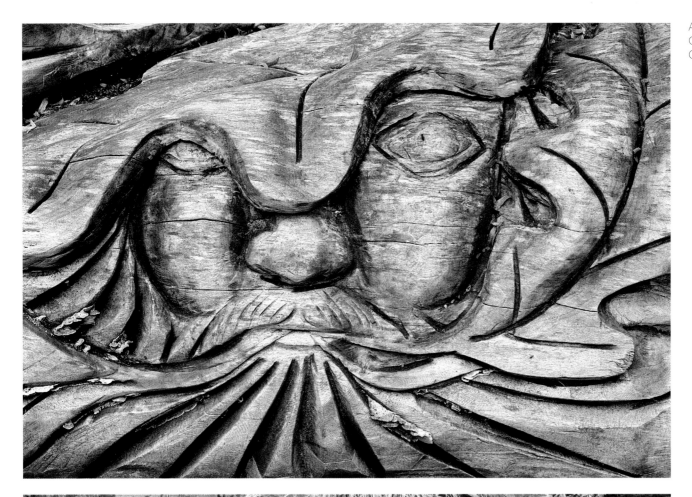

A carved bench near Queen Charlotte's Cottage in the Conservation Area

Water and ferns in the Rock Garden

Rose hips in the
Rose Garden

Wheelbarrows rest after
a hard day's work

the princess of wales conservatory

The Princess of Wales Conservatory was opened by Diana, Princess of Wales, in July 1987. It was named in honour of a previous Princess of Wales: Augusta, wife of Frederick and mother of George III, who is widely accepted as the founder of Kew as a botanical garden. The new conservatory was built to replace twenty-six small, dilapidated glasshouses that were home to a variety of different plants. It was decided to re-house these plants under one roof.

The remit to the architects was to design a building with the highest possible energy efficiency and the lowest possible maintenance costs. It had to be aesthetically pleasing and in harmony with the illustrious buildings, the Palm House and the Orangery, situated near by. Easy!

In fact the architect, Gordon Wilson, did a grand job, designing a state-of-the-art building with ten different climate zones and the latest computer technology controlling the heat and humidity in each zone. Underneath the building is a series of boilers that provide the heat and two huge storage tanks for rainwater, which is collected from the roof and recycled for irrigation and refilling the pond. Sensors on the walls and in the flower beds control window opening and therefore ventilation and increase or decrease the mist sprayed to control the humidity.

The large tree trunk over the main pond is made of concrete with a steel central support, as timber would rot in no time under such conditions. The mould for the model was taken from a felled tree in the Arboretum.

There are two main zones – the wet tropics and the dry tropics – and eight smaller specialist areas.

The dry tropics represent desert areas around the world, where it is hot in the day and cold at night. It includes the collection of Minnerva Sherman Hoyt, an American socialite who dedicated her life to charity work, with special emphasis on the conservation of desert areas and cacti. She had lived in Pasadena and grown to love the desert there. When her son and husband died, she took solace in the desert and set about

trying to protect the area. She was instrumental in getting the land now known as the Joshua Tree National Park designated a protected area. She had a travelling road show of cacti, which she took around the world, educating people about desert environments. She came to England with her collection and instead of returning to America with it she donated it to Kew. The mural near the south entrance of the dry topics zone is a representation of a desert scene with her cacti specimens in the foreground.

The wet tropics zone includes a pond in which grows a giant Amazon waterlily. A small mangrove swamp grows in the boggy soil around the pond's margins. Water dragons are to be released soon to join the lizards already present. These reptiles help keep the insect numbers under control, so minimizing the need to use insecticides.

Each year in February there is a tropical plant and orchid festival. The name orchid comes from the Greek word *orchis*, meaning 'testicle', after the appearance of the plants' subterranean tuberoids. The word *orchis* was first used by Theophrastus in his book *De Historia Plantarum*. A student of Aristotle, he is considered the father of botany. The orchids or Orchidaceae are the largest and most diverse of the flowering plant families. The great majority are found in the tropics, mostly in Asia and South and Central America. There seem to be endless structural variations in the flowers that encourage pollination by particular species of insects, bats or birds. Considering the variety of orchids it is surprising that only one is of commercial importance for food. That is vanilla, the foodstuff flavouring used especially in ice cream. The festival sees the conservatory come alive with a multitude of extravagant displays, all sympathetically arranged to look natural in the surroundings and presenting myriad sizes, shapes and colours of flowers on which to feast your eyes.

Also in the conservatory is a zone full of carnivorous plants. These plants normally live in areas of poor boggy soil and get

Red torch cactus (*Echinopsis huascha*) in the Princess of Wales Conservatory

Sunrise over the Princess of Wales Conservatory

their food from the decomposed insects that have the misfortune to be lured into their deadly traps. Sundews, Venus flytraps and pitcher plants are all present in the cool area on the eastern side of the conservatory.

The north entrance is always home to an exhibition of some sort, which changes at regular intervals throughout the year.

The Palm House: some of the
rusting ironwork inside, and the
view from the Arboretum

the temperate house

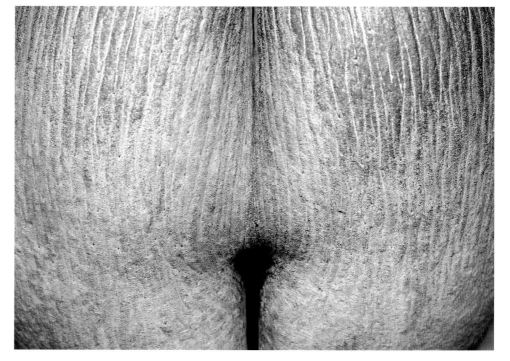

By the mid-eighteenth century it was obvious to Sir William Hooker that another large glasshouse was desperately needed at Kew. Plants were arriving almost daily from the world's temperate zones, brought back by the many plant hunters combing newly discovered lands for interesting specimens. These were plants that did not need the extreme heat and humidity provided by the tropical Palm House but did need protection from the frost, rain and wind of an English winter. Also, the glasshouses built in Joseph Banks's time were falling apart, many of the plants in the Orangery were in a very bad state and some palms in the Palm House were becoming too large for it. Hooker lobbied the government for funds, and after much negotiation these were made available in 1859.

The design for the new Temperate House was by Decimus Burton, architect of the nearby Palm House, but the Temperate House was a very different style of building, much more angular and functional. Cost was a big factor: it was twice as big as the Palm House, which could fit comfortably inside the new glasshouse with room to spare. Gravel from the excavation of the lake was used to provide an elevated podium for it.

The building had a large central area with an octagon on either side and other smaller wings to the north and south. The central area and the octagons were constructed by 1863, but then the money ran out. The original £10,000 had been spent, as well as a further £19,000 – evidently government building projects costs spiralling out of control are not a new phenomenon. The government refused to provide more money and building work stopped. Eventually the building was completed in 1899, when the north and south wings were finished.

As soon as the central house was built, the old greenhouse, the Great Stove, was demolished. A wisteria arch near the Secluded Garden commemorates its position. All the unhappy citrus trees from the Orangery were relocated in the new

Pillars in the Temperate House

Temperate House and the largest palms were transferred from the overcrowded Palm House.

A little over a hundred years later, in 1977, restoration work began. Like the Palm House, the Temperate House is a Grade I listed building and therefore any restoration has to be meticulously careful. The aim was to preserve the essence of the old building while updating and improving the heating and glazing technology. Today the Temperate House is the largest surviving Victorian greenhouse still in existence in the world. It contains the world's largest indoor plant, the Chilean wine palm (*Jubaea chilensis*). This is in the centre of the house, standing fifty-two feet high and still growing. There is a slightly smaller version growing near by to take over when it becomes too large for the building. The rarest plant at Kew also resides in the Temperate House. This is a cycad from South Africa, *Encephalartos woodii*, one of the last surviving specimens in the world.

In winter the temperature in the house is kept at a steady 6–7°C with heat piped there from the boiler house, situated a quarter of a mile away. In summer many of the specimens, especially the fruit trees, are wheeled outside, where they survive the English summer quite happily.

The plants inside the house are arranged in zones, with South African heaths and proteas in the south octagon, plants from New Zealand in the north octagon, Asian plants in the north wing and African plants in the south wing.

Every year the Temperate House provides a spectacular backdrop to the Summer Swing music festival and the winter ice-skating rink.

A reflection in the window of
Museum No.1 sees the sun go
down behind the Palm House.

what is taxonomy?

The year 2007 saw the 300th anniversary of the birth of Carl Linnaeus. He is known as 'the father of taxonomy', which is the study of plant classification. His binomial system is still the template used in plant naming today.

Linnaeus was born in Sweden in 1707. His father was a preacher with a love of horticulture that he indulged as a hobby. Carl, however, loved botany with a passion. He had no desire to follow in his father's footsteps and enter the church. Instead, he studied medicine, which in those days was closely linked to botany because of the extensive knowledge physicians had to have of the plants they used to make healing potions. While studying for his medical degree in the Netherlands, Linnaeus published the first edition of his classification of living things, *Systema Naturae*. He returned to Sweden in 1738 to practise medicine, specializing in the treatment of syphilis (a major problem in the eighteenth century). He was awarded a professorship at Uppsala, where he restored the university's botanical garden, arranging the plants according to his system of classification. This system was based solely on the arrangement of the reproductive organs – a basis that was controversial in its day. Some critics attacked it for its sexually explicit nature; one opponent, botanist John Siegesbeck, called it 'loathesome harlotry'. Linnaeus had his revenge by naming a small, useless European weed 'Siegesbeckia'. He often named plants for his friends: for instance, his colleague Elias Til-Landz had a phobia of water and he chose 'Tillandsia' as the name for air plants that take their moisture from the air and require little water at the roots. He died in 1778 and his only son died five years later, leaving no heirs. His library, manuscripts and natural history collections were sold to the English natural historian Sir James Edward Smith, who founded the Linnean Society in London to take care of them. This society still exists today.

The life's work of this great naturalist was to bring order into the system of naming all living organisms. He gave each plant two names: a genus (usually a noun) and a species epithet (usually an adjective). Set out in his book *Species Planarum* in 1753, this was the binomial system that was the foundation of modern scientific nomenclature.

Plants at Kew have labels that give both the common name and the scientific name. Common names are notoriously unreliable, especially in an international context. In England the 'bluebell' is *Hyacinthoides non-scripta*, a bulb that makes sheets of blue in the woods in the spring; in Scotland, the 'bluebell' is *Campanula rotundifolia*, a small summer flower of open grassland, known in England as the harebell; in Australia, a 'bluebell' is the climber *Sollya heterophylla*. It is vital to use the botanical name when buying a plant. There are 300 types of campanula or bellflower ranging from the delicate three-inch-high rockery variety to six-foot-high towering giants. Which would you prefer on your small balcony?

Plant names are often very descriptive and sometimes enormous fun. For instance, the name *Iris foetidissima* tells you that you wouldn't want it on your living-room table. In Latin, *iris* means 'a rainbow of many colours'; *foetid* means 'smelly', with *issima* meaning 'most'. This plant is commonly known as the stinking iris. The binomial system works well for wild plants, but for cultivated plants, which have been selected and brought into cultivation or deliberately hybridized in gardens and nurseries, a third name is necessary. This name is that of the cultivar or cultivated variety. Some of the names chosen are truly bizarre. What on earth must an *Iris* 'Baboon Bottom' look like? And what prompted the cultivar name of *Hemerocallis* 'Little Bugger'?

A hundred years after Linnaeus, following the work of Darwin and Mendel, with their theories on evolution and genetic inheritance, classification moved on from Linnaeus's grouping of plants by their reproduction organs to reflect evolutionary changes. Nowadays, plants are being grouped according to differences in their genetic fingerprints; with the superior knowledge acquired by DNA research, they are being reclassified in a more accurate way. Plant classification is an ongoing science

The Davies Alpine House at sunset

and Kew is at the forefront of the research, with scientists in the Jodrell Laboratory pioneering techniques using DNA gene sequences and the chemicals that plants naturally produce to reveal relationships between them. Through this and related research the scientists also hope to maximize the abilities of plants to produce food for the world population and to produce medicines to fight global disease.

In the Order Beds at Kew, near the Princess of Wales Conservatory, plants are arranged systematically in family groups to help the visitor and student alike understand taxonomy.

kew: world heritage site

In 1959, the Egyptian government decided to build the Aswan High dam. To do this it had to flood a valley containing treasures of ancient civilizations such as the Abu Simbel temples. The United Nations Educational, Scientific and Cultural Organization (UNESCO) launched a safeguarding campaign. The Temples of Abu Simbel and Philae were taken apart, moved to a higher location and rebuilt. Fifty different countries united and contributed $40 million of the $80 million it cost to complete the project. It was considered a great success and led to other safeguarding schemes, such as saving Venice and its lagoon. UNESCO then initiated a draft convention to protect the cultural heritage to common mankind. In 1972, thirteen years later and after much discussion, a convention concerning the protection of the world cultural and natural heritage was adopted by the general conference.

The convention stated that primarily a country must decide on its own cultural and natural priorities. These were known as the tentative list. Only sites on that list could be put forward to become world heritage sites. Detailed files on the sites are compiled and the site is then nominated and put before the International Council on Monuments and Sites and the World Conservation Union. These two organizations evaluate the merits of the nominated sites and make recommendations to the World Heritage Committee, which meets once a year and decides which sites to select. All sites have to have 'outstanding universal value' and must meet at least one of six selection criteria. In 2006 a total of 830 sites were listed worldwide: 644 cultural, 162 natural and 24 mixed properties.

Kew was nominated in 2002 and inscribed in 2003, meeting not one but three of the selection criteria. It was described as a unique cultural landscape and as having played an important role in landscape and garden history. This description reflects the fact that there are on the site, as well as an ancient monument, more than forty listed structures – many of them iconic buildings that are fine examples of architecture from the Georgian and Victorian eras. Capability Brown, William Chambers and William Nesfield were all highly acclaimed landscape designers/architects who influenced the development of the botanic gardens, their legacy remaining today. The award also acknowledges the work and achievements of past and current generations of scientists and horticulturists, who work tirelessly behind the scenes using knowledge acquired through their research to benefit mankind. As a World Heritage Site, Kew now sits comfortably and deservedly with such illustrious sites as the Pyramids and the Grand Canyon. The award enhanced Kew's global reputation even further.

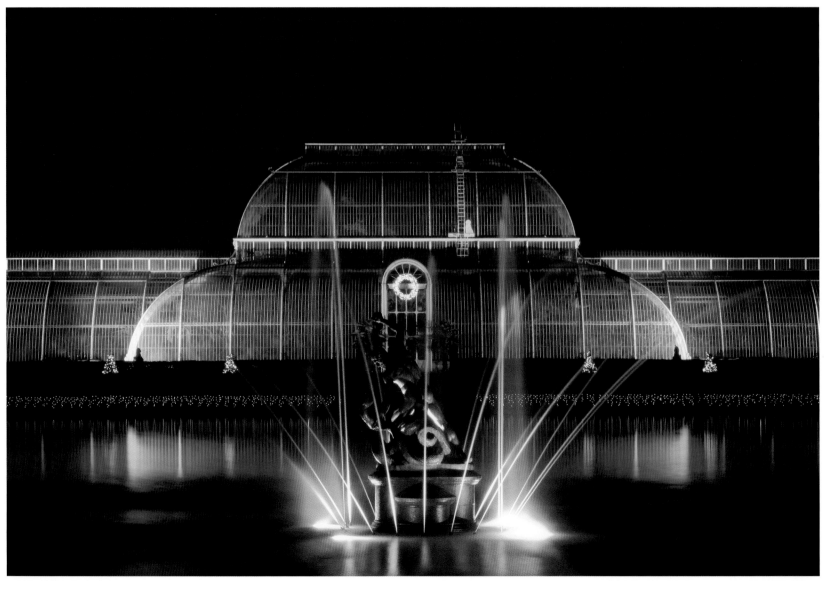

index

Entries in *italics* refer to illustrations